ESOL

DEVELOPING ADULT TEACHING AND LEARNING: PRACTITIONER GUIDES

Melanie Cooke and Celia Roberts

Essex County Council Libraries

(England and Wales)
21 De Montfort Street
Leicester LE1 7GE

Company registration no. 2603322
Charity registration no. 1002775
Published by NIACE in association with NRDC.

NIACE has a broad remit to promote lifelong learning opportunities for adults.
NIACE works to develop increased participation in education and training,
particularly for those who do not have easy access because of class, gender, age,
race, language and culture, learning difficulties or disabilities, or insufficient
financial resources.

For a full catalogue of all NIACE's publications visit
www.niace.org.uk/publications

Cataloguing in Publications Data
A CIP record for this title is available from the British Library
ISBN 978-1-86201-336-0

Cover design by Creative by Design Limited, Paisley
Designed and typeset by Creative by Design Limited, Paisley
Printed and bound by Aspect Binders and Print Ltd

Developing adult teaching and learning: Practitioner guides

This is one of several linked publications arising from the five Effective Practice Studies carried out by the National Research and Development Centre for Adult Literacy and Numeracy (NRDC) from 2003 to 2007.

The five studies explored effective teaching and learning in reading, writing, numeracy, ESOL and using ICT. To date, three series of publications have been produced from the Effective Practice Studies: the research reports and the development project reports, all published by NRDC; and these practitioner guides, published in partnership between NIACE and NRDC.

For more information on the first two series, please see **www.nrdc.org.uk**

Contents

Acknowledgements

This guide was co-authored by:

- Patrick Bushell
- Michael Hepworth
- James McGoldrick
- Jim O'Neill

With contributions from:

- Karen Dudley
- Anna Goodband

Peer review

This guide has been peer reviewed. The critical readers were:

- John Callaghan, University of Leeds
- John Sutter, LLU+, London South Bank University

How to use this guide

The guide is divided into five sections. If you don't have time to read it all – although we hope you will! – then each section, except the introduction, stands alone. For this reason some of the guidelines for teachers are the same in each section.

Section 2 is a general one on opening up spaces for learners to talk; section 3 is about speaking at Entry 1; Section 4 is about standard western narratives (Labov, 1972) and is probably useful for people teaching classes at Entry 3 and above; the final section deals with argumentation and will be appropriate for Levels 1 and 2. However, we hope that any narrow interpretation of 'level' in curricula and language learning textbooks will be challenged by this guide, so please experiment and try things out at other levels too. Each section describes the action research cycle as experienced by one of the teachers, and each one provides a set of suggestions for you to follow if you want to try something similar yourself. The sections all end with a list of further reading for those who wish to find out more.

1 | **Background and context**

Before, our tongues were heavy and we didn't know what to say. Now they are light and I feel my tongue can fly. (ESOL student, Turning Talk into Learning Project)

Introduction

This guide is about finding ways of turning learner talk into opportunities for teaching and learning. It is based on an action research project inspired by some of the findings from the ESOL Effective Practice Project (EEPP). These are described in detail in *Effective Teaching and Learning: ESOL* (Baynham and Roberts *et al.*, 2007). One of the conclusions from that research study was:

One of [teachers'] *main tasks is to encourage classroom talk, transforming talk into learning and learning into talk. This is the result both of long-term planning and the 'online' planning which occurs when teachers act responsively and contingently as each moment unfolds in the classroom.* (p. 54)

This guide describes the experiences of four teachers as they explored the kind of talk their learners produced in class and ways of building on that talk to help the learners become more effective speakers of English. It also helps ESOL (English for Speakers of other Languages) teachers to develop their analysis of learner talk and gives ideas of how they can do this kind of research themselves in their own teaching contexts.

The ESOL Effective Practice Project (EEPP)

The main findings from the final report of the EEPP, which we drew on for this guide, are:

- ESOL learners have few opportunities to speak English in their daily lives, so tend to favour classrooms which are interactive and have a strong focus on speaking. The need to interact in a language in order to learn it is established in Second Language Acquisition (SLA) theory. Interaction is also important for Second Language Socialisation, i.e. the process whereby people new to a community learn the ways of being of that community.

- Most classrooms observed for the EEPP showed effective teaching and learning taking place. The most common ways this was achieved was through creating a supportive environment, employing direct teaching strategies such as modelling and repeating, planning, and creating balance and variety in lessons. However, the most effective teachers in the study also drew on learners' own experiences and lives outside the classroom – bringing the outside in – and, crucially, encouraged them to 'speak from within'. We observed that where learners were speaking from within they produced longer, more complex stretches of talk, which we know to be essential for language learning and acquisition to take place.

- Explicitness was a major strength of many effective teachers. Raising awareness of linguistic structures helps learners to notice language. This is also established as an important aspect of SLA.

- The effective classrooms were oriented to adults and their interests. This means stretching students beyond their current competence and concerns and involving them in topics that are intellectually challenging.

- We saw fewer classrooms which encouraged learners to be reflective, evaluative or critical, and few lessons which focused on spoken language at the level of discourse.

In this action research project, then, we wished to expand on some of the effective teaching we observed on the EEPP, in particular to combine the strengths of planning and explicitness with the need to respond to learner talk as it arises, either spontaneously or as part of the lesson plan. We wanted to focus on talk at the level of discourse (i.e. above the word/simple sentence level), even at Entry 1, and to explore what our learners might need to know to become more effective at producing longer utterances and at participating in conversations and other interactions. We also wanted to explore which topics our learners wanted to talk about and what stories they had to tell if given the right opportunities to do so.

Action research

This project followed several principles from exploratory teaching practice (as described by Allwright and Bailey, 1991) and from action research; this is described fully in Cooke and Roberts (2007). The cycle we followed is shown in Figure 1.

1. Explore and reflect
Reflect on own practices when responding to learner talk. Set up opportunities for learners to speak, and notice how we respond to them.

2. Plan
Record some stretches of learner talk, transcribe and analyse it. Plan a series of lessons based on the analysis.

4. Analyse and reflect
Analyse and evaluate the changes that have happened as a result of your own action. Reflect on new puzzles arising from your new data.

3. Act
Teach the first lesson. Record and transcribe some learner talk. Redesign next lessons if necessary, to respond to learner talk. Discuss and write up findings. Start process again...

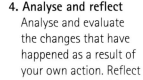

Figure 1: The action research cycle.

Turning talk into learning: Principles for ESOL classrooms

The following are guidelines we developed for this project which you could follow if you wish to work with real learner talk:

- If a student comes to class with a need to communicate, allow space for the story, problem, anecdote, request or query; in other words respond contingently to learners' real-life experiences as and when they bring them to the ESOL classroom. This will open up unexpected and valuable learning opportunities.

- As the EEPP report pointed out, 'talk is work' in the ESOL classroom. Much talk is conversation, so it is essential for learners to gain conversational competence. 'Conversationalise' your pedagogy where possible/appropriate by building in time for talk, encouraging learners to respond to and comment on classroom activities and make links with their knowledge and experience.

- Stretch learners beyond their prescribed linguistic level. Learners at Entry 1 need to 'speak from within' and express the same things as higher-level learners and should not be held back from doing so until they have acquired certain grammatical forms (see Section 3 for more on this).

- Don't focus only on the most noticeable errors in learner talk, such as missing 'ed' endings, which rarely impede communication. In many cases a look at a transcript will show that it is something else that is causing problems for the listener, such as how the learner organises a standard western narrative (see Sections 3 and 4 for more on this).

- Make judicious decisions about when to correct a learner. It is often inappropriate to correct when someone has an urgent need to express themselves.

- One finding from this project was that learners tend to listen to each other more if they are focusing on each others' meanings. If their talk is valued and used as pedagogic material, learners will get into the habit of listening more in class.

- Encourage learners to set the agenda in speaking activities, e.g. picking the topic. Research has shown that when a topic is brought up by a learner it is more memorable than if it is 'imposed' by the teacher or teaching materials.

- Be willing to let go of your lesson plan when necessary, at least for parts of your lesson. Build in some unstructured time in your plan in which you encourage and respond to learner talk.

- Be prepared to take some risks with topics. Allow learners to initiate and explore topics which you may consider 'difficult' or sensitive, or which simply may not have occurred to you.

- Be prepared to do some work outside the classroom when you come to analyse your learners' talk. You will need to transcribe stretches of talk, and consult books or other professionals about your findings and how to analyse them. This might appear onerous if you have a heavy workload but the benefit for you will be to re-invigorate your teaching and enhance your motivation.

- Discuss your work as often as possible with people who are doing the same thing.

The scope of this guide

There is a long academic tradition in linguistics which informs much second-language pedagogy. Teaching 'speaking' is a huge, complex endeavour and we can only touch very briefly on certain approaches to it here. We know that teachers generally have a thorough introduction in their teacher training programmes to aspects of speaking such as pronunciation, accuracy/fluency and the whys and wherefores of correction. We also presume that teachers have some exposure to the major approaches to language teaching such as Task-based Learning and Communicative Language Teaching, and to pedagogic speaking activities such as role-plays and dialogues. In this guide, therefore, we have chosen to focus on those aspects of teaching speaking which are less often covered in initial teacher training (ITT) and continuing professional development (CPD).

Using transcriptions

In this project we transcribed stretches of learner talk which provided us with ideas for learner-centred lessons (called 'Extracts'). Transcription is a powerful tool; focusing on talk (yours as well as your learners') as you transcribe helps you to notice and think about communication features you would otherwise miss. The process of transcription makes the talk interesting and brings it alive. There are many levels of detail at which you can transcribe, depending on what you wish to show. You can decide for yourself, for example, if you need to find a way to show intonation or body language. The following is a key to the tapescripts in this guide, which you may use or adapt as you think fit:

Key to transcriptions

(.)	Brief pause
(2 secs)	Timed pause
(he's)	Transcription uncertain: a guess
( )	Unclear speech: not transcribed
Okay **Yes please**	Overlapping speech
[ ]	Paralinguistic features, e.g. *laughter*

From Graddol *et al.* (1994).

If you want to find out more

Research for teachers

Allwright, D. and Bailey, K.D. (1991) *Focus on the Language Classroom: An introduction to classroom research for language teachers.* Cambridge: Cambridge University Press.

McNiff, J. and Whitehead, J. (2005) *Action Research for Teachers: A Practical Guide.* London: David Fulton Publishers.

Wallace, M.J. (1998) *Action Research for Language Teachers.* Cambridge: Cambridge University Press.

Working with spoken language

Cameron, D. (2001) *Working with Spoken Discourse.* London: Sage.

Seedhouse, P. (2005) *The Interactional Architecture of the Language Classroom: A Conversation Analysis Perspective.* Oxford: Blackwell.

Walsh, S. (2006) *Investigating Classroom Discourse.* London: Routledge.

Second language acquisition

Block, D. (2003) *The Social Turn in Second Language Acquisition.*
    Edinburgh: Edinburgh University Press.

Second language socialisation

Zuengler, J. and Cole, K. (2004) 'Language socialisation and second
    language learning'. In: E. Hinkel (ed.) *Handbook of Research in Second
    Language Teaching and Learning.* New Jersey: Lawrence Earlbaum
    Associates.

2 Turning talk into learning: Opening up interactional spaces

Something which I like doing ... is not bombarding students with materials. I have worked in places where people just got by by dishing out worksheet after worksheet ... [they] hide behind a lot of material. (Jim, EEPP project)

Introduction

This section is about:

- opening up interactional spaces in the classroom;
- responding contingently to learners when they bring the 'outside' into the classroom; and
- making your lessons more authentically 'learner-centred'.

Opening up spaces for talk

In the course of the EEPP project we observed many instances of teachers closing down the spaces for interaction that learners were trying to open up, either because of a wish to stick to the lesson plan or to avoid sensitive issues. There is a sharp contrast in the amount and quality of learner talk in lessons in which this happens and those in which the teacher responds contingently to learners' immediate concerns.

Carol's class

In this extract from a class in outer London, Carol, the teacher, responds to a real-life story told by her learners at the beginning of the lesson. Melinda is normally a shy, hesitant speaker, but despite this she initiates a recount of something which happened to her the day before:

Extract 1: The tram (from Carol's E3 ESOL class, EEPP)
(M = Melinda; D = Dalia; T = teacher; S3 = third
student; Ss = students)

1. **M:** Yesterday I left my children in the tram **they didn't**
2. **T:** **Tram**
3. **M:** The tram closed the door I leave my children inside
4. **T:** [*intake of breath signalling shock*]
5. **D:** Yesterday I saw you you get down
6. **T:** What, Dalia was getting off?
7. **D:** Yeah getting off, out
8. **M:** I am inside my children both out
9. **T:** So you were left on the tram and your children
10. **M:** Out
11. **T:** Were on the pavement
12. **M:** Yeah
13. **T:** What did you do?
14. **M:** They are shouting I shouting but the tram is starting yeah
15. **T:** But can you
16. **D:** There is a was a button you can er speak with the driver
17. **M:** Yeah but the (   ) somebody's there but he can't stop it
18. **T:** So did you shout to the driver?
19. **M:** Yeah
20. **T:** And what did he do?
21. **M:** I waiting last the box, the tram box I shout but he didn't (   )
22. **T:** So you shouted into the box? Was it an intercom?
23. **D:** Yeah, yeah you know that
24. **T:** I haven't seen one I haven't been on a tram

"Carol's lessons show her taking these stories and weaving them into the fabric of the learning."

25. **D:** It's new information for you

26. **T:** Yes! I'm learning every time, every lesson I learn something

27. **D:** And sometimes the ticket machine doesn't work, yes the help point machine there you press the button and they er speak with you and say four digit number give to you, you go to tram with the four digit number and then the checking people coming you tell the four digit number and they don't

28. **S3:** They don't er

29. **T:** They don't charge you or fine you

30. **D:** Yes, yes

31. **T:** Is this on the tram or when you're trying to buy a ticket

32. **D:** When you're trying to buy a ticket on another side there's a help machine

33. **T:** A help point

34. **D:** Yes

35. **S3:** A help point

36. **T:** And do you speak to somebody

37. **D:** Yes

38. **T:** Oh it's a real person

39. **D:** Yes yes they speak

40. **T:** That's amazing. A real person, not a tape

41. **M:** Yes ( ) £10 is taking machine then I phoned the point I can't get a ticket

42. **T:** You pressed the buzzer

43. **M:** Yeah yeah then the tram come to East Croydon and I get the ticket and no come ( ) money

44. **T:** You had to pay

45. **M:** Yeah the machine is £10 taking and I take ticket

46. **T:** Did you get the change? You didn't get the change? So tell me, did you get your children back?

47. **M:** Yeah, yeah [laughs]

48. **T:** Good! [laughs] oh that's worrying isn't it?

49. **Ss:** Mmm

50. **T:** Oh dear

51. **M:** Next stop I ( ) last stop I get off and back one stop

52. **T:** [laughs] So you've done all your keep fit for the week?

This stretch of talk demonstrates what learners might produce when given the space to do so. Here Carol, Dalia and Melinda construct together a narrative (see Sections 3 and 4) and a description of how something works (turn 27 onwards). The teacher is provided with a lot to work with here, and indeed Carol's lessons show her taking these stories and weaving them into the fabric of the learning, returning to them through the course of a lesson and even across lessons. This creates a sense amongst learners that their talk is important (thereby creating more talk) and also a need for learners to listen to each other as they will be called upon at a later moment to tell their own stories and respond to those told earlier.

James's class

During the exploratory phase of this action research project the team was asked to provide as many opportunities as possible for learners to talk. During this phase, James made the following notes as he tried to open up spaces for interaction in the classroom, and to respond contingently to his learners, i.e. as and when they initiated talk, especially unplanned talk:

> This is a complex area for me as I am somebody who actually likes to write lesson plans. Why do I like lesson plans? I like thinking things through. The process of writing the lesson is almost like a mini rehearsal for the lesson, giving me confidence and helping me to remember the stages and activities. Is it also something to do with working in FE, where evidence is everything and lesson plans are an institutional demand? I like the structure they provide, the lesson is mapped out for me – and the learners – and there seems a point or purpose. However, as a result of the initial lessons and my reflections I was aware of the need to allow learners to control topicalisation, which to some extent might require a 'letting go of the lesson plan'! This means being 'freer' and 'going with the teachable moment' (Condelli et al., 2003); being more agendaless. In this project I wanted to experiment with ... 'letting talk happen' and see if I could do anything with it.

James therefore decided to allow extended unplanned talk, if the opportunity arose, which it does here when a student, Arturo, arrives late and explains why:

Extract 2: The bank account (Level 2 speaking class)
A = Arturo; N = Nadia; E = Elly; B = Belinda;
C = Clarissa; T = Teacher

1. **A:** Yeah, I was in bank and I got stuck there

2. **T:** You got stuck in the bank? The long queue?

3. **N:** This is my problem.

4. **A:** No no, my case, was complicated so

5. **T:** I think that's one thing, the banks have got so bad here. There never used be queues in the bank like there are now. Where you know when you can queue out the door

6. **A:** But you know maybe it's because of foreigners and they don't really know how to treat because they ask me of course for proof of address and I had letter from the family

7. **T:** Yeah

8. **A:** Explaining that either of had this kind of bank account

9. **E:** You wanted to open an account?

10. **A:** Yeah and then

11. **B:** You have contract with?

12. **A:** Because they offer me er 'passport bank account'. This is the name of this service. But you have to pay every month

13. **N:** For what?

14. **A:** I said 'No, I want free' [*laughs*]

15. **T:** But did you get what you wanted in the end?

16. **A:** Yeah. We will see. Because this man – he wasn't convinced. But anyway, he said he would send to the centre or somewhere and they would apply

17. **N:** To the address to see if you are there. They want to send you the form to your address to see if you live if you really live there or something

18. **A:** Ah maybe

19. **N:** Yeah. You have to check first

20. **B:** Yeah. You need something

21. **T:** Oh right.

22. **A:** I live there, so [*laughs*]

23. **C:** I didn't have any problem with this account

24. **T:** Didn't you?

25. **B:** Yeah it's really complicated

26. **C:** I opened it after two months when I came here

27. **B:** But you need a contract, you need take your passport, you need to

28. **C:** I had passport and my bank account from my country with address here

29. **A:** And but it's for free?

[Continues for some minutes more]

James notes the following about this episode:

*I prompted a little but tried to let the learners develop the conversation and participate in some 'real' opinion giving – allowing them 'interactional space' to develop the talk and take control or turn taking. The learners were all speaking quickly and relatively loudly throughout this exchange indicating engagement and a real need to share opinion. There is also some jostling for 'floor-holding'. At the end of the interaction I briefly focused on some of the vocabulary which had come up 'to be black-listed', 'credit rating' etc. I didn't do much more than this but it did seem to be a significant episode. **I had previously put a lot of effort into thinking of tasks which would encourage learners to have these kinds of discussions, which often ended up feeling false and contrived.***

"I had previously put a lot of effort into creating tasks to promote discussion which ended up feeling false and contrived."

Conclusion – Spaces

James's final point is a key one in this guide and one which was borne out by the other teachers on the team. Responding to learners contingently as Carol and James do here gives many unexpected opportunities for language learning, as well as a wealth of ideas for future lessons, both linguistically and in terms of topic. James would not have been so aware of this had he not been involved with this project, or had not transcribed some stretches of classroom interaction.

Even when the topic or activity is more teacher controlled there will be many opportunities to 'conversationalise' (Thornbury and Slade, 2006) the learning. In the EEPP project there were many instances of rich learner talk around texts, for example, in which teachers drew skilfully on their learners' socio-cultural and linguistic knowledge, as well as examples of creative activities and tasks which encouraged learners to take risks, produce longer stretches of talk and work

Try it out

- Allow the outside in: if a student comes to class with a need to communicate, allow space for the story, problem, anecdote, request or query. Involve other students. Make the 'learner talk' the subject of the lesson. Follow it up with action, if necessary (a letter to the local councillor, a trip out into the local community and so on).

- Bring the outside in: ask students to bring in texts and topics they find interesting, puzzling, infuriating or important. Allow this to become the curriculum, if not all the time then once a week or once a month. The work of Elsa Auerbach on the 'participatory curriculum' is useful for ideas and strategies for this kind of teaching.

- Encourage learners to notice language they hear around them and bring along examples to discuss in class. In this project James asked his Level 2 learners to keep a diary of idioms which amused, attracted or baffled them. They then used these as a workshop to teach each other what they had noticed during the week in their workplaces and daily lives. This could work for many areas of language, such as speech acts (e.g. apologising, greeting, leave-taking etc), local varieties (e.g. dialect, accent) and so on.

- Set aside regular time for 'talking circles' (Ernst in Thornbury and Slade, 2006) in which learners share news, anecdotes experiences and special events. Learners are responsible for initiating conversations and topic shifts.

- Encourage learners to get used to being recorded and where possible use their own stretches of talk for analysis and modelling (see section 5 for an example of this).

- Ask learners to keep a learning diary (in whatever language they wish) of the times outside the lesson when they want to communicate something but are unable to. They should record which kind of interaction it was, and what they would have liked to say, or why they think they did not get positive results in their interaction (e.g. on the phone, in service encounters, trying to explain a problem, chatting to neighbours and so on). Use these to explore the social, cultural and political contexts of the language use of your students.

- If students speak little English in their daily lives, make this a point of discussion and reflection in class. Why? What are the social forces at play that create this situation? What could be done to enhance speaking opportunities for learners within your institutions?

"Ask Learners to keep a diary, in whatever language, of when they want to say something but can't express it."

If you want to find out more

Auerbach, E.R. (1992) *Making Meaning, Making Change*. USA: Centre for Applied Linguistics and ERIC.

Baynham, M. (2007) 'Agency and contingency in the language learning of refugees and asylum seekers', Special Issue, *Linguistics and Education*, Vol. 17 No. 1: 24–39.

Kumaravadivelu, B. (2003) *Macrostrategies for Language Teaching*. Yale University Press.

Thornbury, S. and Slade, D. (2006) *Conversation: From Description to Pedagogy*. Cambridge: Cambridge University Press.

Tsui, A.B.M. (1995) *Introducing Classroom Interaction*. London: Penguin.

van Lier, L. (1996) *Interaction in the Language Curriculum: Awareness, Autonomy and Authenticity*. Harlow: Longman.

Turning talk into learning at Entry 1

together to construct conversations even at low levels.

> *There's not much for students to discuss or – there are useful things in there but I*
> *don't know what they learn about the world around them, apart from how to read*
> *a bus timetable or to buy something in a shop ... which I think is a bit of a shame.*
> (Dora, EEPP, talking about ESOL *Skills for Life* materials for Entry 1)

Introduction

This section is about:

- ■ encouraging learners at Entry 1 to produce longer stretches of talk, beyond word or simple sentence level;
- ■ moving beyond controlled practice; and
- ■ discovering what learners like to talk about.

Jim's class

Exploratory stage

For this action research project Jim chose to work with learners at Entry 1. His class were young students (16–19 year olds) from Somalia, Bangladesh, Afghanistan, Kurdistan, Iran and Pakistan. During the first phase of the research, Jim recorded several lessons in which he set up activities to encourage learners to talk. One activity he tried was adapted from a board game called 'Tell Us About', from a book called *Keep Talking* by Friederike Klippel (1984). The players throw a dice and move round the board. When they land on a square they have to talk about whatever is written on that square (e.g. a TV programme you like, something you would like to possess). In this lesson there were nine students. For this activity they worked in groups of three for about 20 minutes. Following is an extract from one of these activities: Student 1 has landed on a square asking her to talk about the weather.

Extract 1: The weather

1.	**S1**:	What's the weather today?	*Falling intonation*
2.	**S2**:	What's the weather	
3.	**S3**:	My country Turkey (.) is very very nice	
4.	**S1**:	Why?	*Rising intonation*
5.		(2 secs)	
6.	**S3**:	Is good	*Emphatic*
7.	**S2**:	London (.) is cold Yeah (.) no like	
8.	**S1**:	Yes	*Signals end of topic*
9.	**S1**:	Another one	
10.	**S2**:	Six	*Casts the die*
11.	**S3**:	No	
12.	**S1**:	Yes (.) one two three four five six	
13.	**S2**:	Where are you live	*Speaking prompt =*
14.	**S1**:	Where are you live	*'where you live'*
15.	**S3**:	Where you live	
16.	**S2**:	My I live in (Walthamstow)	
17.	**S3**:	(3 secs) OK me I take	*Takes turn*

As the extract shows, when Jim's students played this game, their turns remained extremely short and were low on anecdotes and description. They seemed more concerned with getting through the game to the end than with telling each other things. After discussion with the action research team, Jim decided he would focus on two things in the second phase of the research:

- Extending learner utterances.
- Finding less formulaic ways to get students talking to see if the same issue (limited utterances) still applied.

Extending learner utterances

In the two follow-up lessons Jim used the same adapted board game format and tried some techniques to get the learners giving/asking for extended information. He tried improving their talk in the game via controlled practice:

■ Setting a 30-second time limit for speaking on a topic (pairs). In this 30-second period the listeners were not allowed to contribute.

■ Controlled practice of a small number of question-heads such as 'How often do you...?', 'Do you like...?', 'What is/are your favourite...?' and so on. These were dealt with as lexical phrases rather than generative grammatical patterns.

■ Always responding with 'Why?' if a speaker says 'I like'.

■ Extending simple statements by continuing with 'because'.

After Jim's controlled practice elements had been implemented, we can see that the learners are now asking each other for extended information and producing longer turns than before:

Extract 2: Computers

Throwing dice for next turn

1. **S5**: Four
2. **S4**: One two three four

   Moving counter, lands on square saying 'computers'

3. **S5**: Four (.) computers
4. **S5**: Are you do you like computers? (.)

   Do you like computer?   *Self-corrects*
5. **S4**: Of course why not?

   (2 secs)

   Because I like computer, sometimes I am (.) I am sometimes understand (.) I use internet I use the internet (.) I like computer

                   Both laughing
6. **S5** Do you have computer?
7. **S4**: Yes is in my house (.) is computer

   No in my house

   Is no computer my computer is my another friend (.) I haven't got any   *Emphatic*

Extract 3: Do you like...

1.	**T**:	Ahmed that means you can ask Khaled any question	*Explains 'free question' on board game*
2.	**S6**:	Do you like do you like (.) country	
3.	**S7**:	Yes I like this country	
4.	**S6**:	Why?	
5.	**S7**:	Because this country very nice and (.) here I'm study before I don't under - don't study	
6.	**S5**:	How long you in er country	
7.	**S6**:	Five months	
8.	**S5**:	Do you like college?	*Second 'free question'*
9.	**S6**:	Yes I love college	
10.	**S7**:	Why?	
11.	**S6**:	Because study in your life very important	

However, the interaction shown here is still somewhat forced and stilted, and still has the flavour of some kind of performance produced at the teacher's behest. It is not coming from the actual experiences of the learners themselves nor from any urge they might have to communicate. In addition, some of the language they have been prompted to use in this task, such as 'do you like...', 'how often do you...', although appearing on most beginner syllabi and expected for their assessments, does not produce particularly convincing-sounding English interaction. Jim was still left looking for more; for the learners to produce more and to be stretched further.

Learners' stories

Jim therefore went on to see if he could create the right environment for his learners to produce longer utterances in what he calls 'more realistic contexts that occur within the classroom environment'.

Jim writes the following:

Thus for the second area of focus, I chose to get them telling stories. I did entertain the idea of just saying to them 'you have ten minutes just to talk together, anything you like' but I decided that this would not meet group expectations of being guided by the teacher. I decided it would be more subtle to prompt some retelling of something I knew had occurred, and of which they had shared knowledge.

The group had recently been on a trip to the Natural History Museum, and I knew of an incident in which one learner had become separated from the group. It was the retelling of this incident that I prompted, with no preference for who would lead the narrative, and no attempt to 'share' the narrative equally. Thereafter, I turned the talk to animals in the museum, and then stories about animals that had occurred in their own lives. At this point, I did ensure each learner took a turn.

The 'a story about animals' narrative was remarkable in that the weakest learner in terms of oral ability absolutely dominated; by the end he had narrated three separate incidents. This shows us the high value of learner-centred lessons for maximising motivation and encouraging meaningful participation.

> "it was remarkable that the weakest learner in oral ability absolutely dominated the storytelling."

An extract from this lesson is shown below:

Extract 4: The snake
A = Abdul; T = Teacher

1.	**T:**	So tell me tell me another story (.) something about animals in your country maybe (.) or in England (.) something which happened	*Following our discussion about animals seen on recent trip*
2.	**A:**	This uncle Before (.) I maybe eight year old ( )	
3.	**T:**	Yeah	
4.	**A:**	I go my house (.) outside (.) I no see of I just walk [phiiiish] Just I [phiiiish] I see (.) I just put my hand up is miss	*Makes noise as part narrative – gestures to show the snake lunging*
5.	**T:**	Yeah	
6.	**A:**	I go back	
7.	**T:**	Uh-hmnn	
8.	**A:**	No my (.) another my another house = not my house	
9.	**T:**	Yeah	
10.	**A:**	Builder (.) builder work yeah I tell him coming coming is big snake snake is people (.) stick bom	*Gestures for hitting the snake with a stick – all laugh*

This anecdote was followed by a series of vivid stories; one long one about a snake, another about a hyena and one about camels eating children. One student who had no animal story told a tale of when he nearly drowned. Jim found the richness of these stories surprising and fascinating and in marked contrast to those produced by his attempts to get them talking in previous lessons. It is evident from these examples that the learners had effective communication resources from their expert languages, such as gesture and mime, which they used to maximum effect. Most importantly, the stories led Jim as a teacher to making a real difference to learner talk, as he wrote in his final reflections: 'discourse patterns, yes discourse patterns at Entry 1'. Here Jim explains what the improvement in discourse patterns consisted of:

> Another noteworthy feature of the story telling was the success of the narrative without any past tense use. However, the narrative did founder when the narrator wanted to move on to another story, but had not rounded off the previous story. He needed to summarise or evaluate (fixed expressions 'I felt/was' plus an adjective did the job nicely in my follow-up lessons) but had not done so. The result was a temporary breakdown in communication (evidenced by an increase in pauses).

> With this particular group, at the stage of the year we were at, I would normally have focused on formulaic interaction patterns to help the learners get through their external accreditation. Instead, I found myself leading them towards complete discourse patterns for narrating stories. This is not found on the current curriculum until Entry 3; here we saw the need for it at Entry 1.

There are clear parallels here to the research done on standard western narrative by Patrick Bushell, which we discuss in section 4 of this guide. The same pattern of discourse identified and worked on with Patrick's higher-level group is relevant and important to a group working towards Entry 1.

Planning with confidence

Learner-centred teaching of this kind can sometimes be seen as incompatible with prescribed curricula and schemes of work which teachers need to write in advance. Indeed, this is one of the objections raised by teachers in discussion of this type of teaching approach, especially at inspection time when they know they will be asked to provide 'evidence' of learning taking place in the period of one lesson. However, Jim himself was observed by an inspector during one of the preliminary sessions in the research cycle for this project. On the lesson plan the fourth objective for the session was given as:

> Learners will be able to: show progress in one area of speaking – not yet identified.

The lesson received an outstanding grade with positive feedback on the speaking outcome which had been left undefined on the plan. This means that the space created on the lesson plan for Jim to respond to learners and adapt accordingly was recognised within the context of this inspection as contributing to effective teaching and learning.

Conclusion – Entry 1

The transcripts from Jim's last lesson and some from the EEPP show that with support (such as questions and scaffolding) from their peers and teacher, Entry 1 learners are able to produce extended utterances and tell stories when they speak 'from within' about topics which interest and motivate them. They also show that what students are interested in is highly unpredictable and often far removed from some of the more predictable ESOL topics of problems in the home or illnesses and so on. Activities and texts brought in by the teacher might be enjoyable but might never reveal the kind of stories that Jim's class produced in the last lesson of this cycle.

Try it out

The following are steps you might follow if you want to try to work with learner talk at Entry 1:

- In all lessons: if a student comes to the class with an urgent need to communicate something, allow her/him space and time to tell the story and work with that, or set aside a 15–20-minute slot on your lesson plan in which you invite students to talk. Identify what kind of things learners are struggling to say, e.g. tell anecdotes, stories, explain problems, describe a situation.

- In the next lesson create a longer space in which learners are invited to produce more of the types of talk you identified in lesson 1. Think of ways in which you might encourage learners to produce the kinds of talk you wish to focus on. This might be planned (as in the game Jim used) or less planned (think of a scary story, tell me about..., what do you think of ...).

- Give learners time to reflect, plan and rehearse their talk and ask for one or two (or all if you have time) to give their anecdote, story etc. Identify what they need to help them be more effective in their communication, both as 'tellers' and listeners.

■ Go away and think about what might be needed to make your learners more effective. This will require you as the teacher to reflect on your own language use and maybe to refer to the second language teaching literature. In the examples above, Jim identified the need for his learners to be able to round off a story and yield the floor to another speaker, so he taught them 'I felt/was plus adjective...' in order to help them do this, but he ignored the lack of past tenses for the time being. Remember, that the obvious teachable features such as 'ed' endings are not always the most important barriers to communication. In standard western narratives and recounts, other issues such as sequence, adverbs of time and structure are more important than verb morphology. Other features at this level might include questions, especially 'why', which enable listeners to interact with the story-teller.

■ Devise a series of lessons or activities based on your reflections on your learners' talk.

And so on...

If you want to find out more

Carter, R. (2003) 'The grammar of talk: spoken English, grammar and the classroom'. In: *New Perspectives on Spoken English in the Classroom*. London: QCA.

Labov, W. (1972) *Language in the Inner City*. Oxford: Basil Blackwell.

van Lier, L. (2001) 'Constraints and resources in classroom talk: Issues of equality and symmetry'. In: C. Candlin and N. Mercer (eds) *English Language Teaching in its Social Context*. London: Routledge.

4 Turning talk into learning: Narratives

I'm happy to take risks in a classroom... someone will have something to say. Or something happens. There's always something...today there was an accident and the roadworks and a crying student. Then it was a lost key. So there's a story behind everything. And that gives me a lesson. (Carol, EEPP)

Introduction

This section is about:

- making the structure of standard western narratives explicit to learners;
- helping learners to analyse examples of spoken English narratives;
- giving learners time to plan and rehearse;
- transferring classroom talk to real-life situations.

The importance of narratives

In the previous section we saw that even learners at Entry 1 have stories they wish to tell in English, and there are several reasons to help ESOL learners become more effective at this. Narratives come in many forms, such as recounts, anecdotes, excuses, exempla (telling a story to show a moral point) and so on, and make up a huge part of everyday conversation. They have a strong performance function, in that much of our identity is constructed through how we present ourselves in the stories we tell and how we tell them. In addition, they also occur in more formal, institutional interactions such as interviews for employment (Roberts and Campbell, 2006) and in very high-stakes interviews such as those asylum seekers are forced to undergo to prove their asylum stories are real (Maryns, 2005).

Patrick's class

Exploratory stage

For this action research project Patrick chose to work with a group of learners who were on a course called 'Speak Clearly'. These learners were on full-time courses at around Entry 3/Level 1, and had been recommended by their tutors to focus specifically on their speaking skills. In the first cycle of the project, Patrick had not yet identified narratives as his focus. Like Jim, his main concern at the beginning, exploratory stage of the cycle was to get his learners to produce extended talk which he could then use to analyse and work with in the rest of the project. In order to do this, Patrick set up a series of speaking activities such as pronunciation, work on spoken discourse markers, such as 'anyway' and presentations. He also factored in the following free speaking activity based on topic cards:

> The idea for the topic card activity was that a group of students (three or four) were given a set of cards with prompts relating to one topic, such as 'shopping' or 'education' etcetera. My instructions were for each student in turn to take one topic, read the prompt and speak for one minute without being interrupted while other students kept time. At the end of the minute the other students were encouraged to continue the topic by adding to it from their own experience before they chose to move to the next.

Overleaf is an example of the kind of learner talk Patrick recorded during this activity:

Extract 1: Jobs

1. **A:** Who's going to speak the first?
2. **B:** Your first job, OK, it's me
3. **C:** But you have to, er, speak just one minute
4. **A:** OK
5. **D:** You start?
6. **B:** My first job was er, I worked at the bank, the European bank in my country, and erm, I worked part time, I worked there one and half year, then I changed my work. I went to the central bank. It's higher. Who's next?
7. **A:** And here, your job?
8. **B:** I don't have a job here
9. **A:** My first job was in hotel, Germany
10. **B:** Next one, you need to change
11. **A:** You need to change?
12. **B:** Yes. You need to change every time   *Takes next card*
13. **B:** It's bad job....You have to
14. **A:** I don't know how to talk but er take care of old people
15. **B:** It's a hard work
16. **A:** It's a hard work and sometimes the other (people?) ... are stupid
17. **B:** Yeah, it's old and they don't understand
18. **A:** They behave like children
19. **B:** Bad than children, sometimes   *Laugh*
20. **B:** OK who's next?

This activity was not particularly successful in encouraging learners to extend their utterances, tell stories and get practice at longer turns. Topics which would ordinarily produce standard western narratives, such as 'the worst job you ever had', were only being touched upon, while other students, like Jim's in section 3, seemed to be more interested in getting to the end of the time limit for the next turn to arrive.

Narrative structures

However, a lot of theoretical work has been done on narratives which we can adapt and draw on to teach ESOL learners. The sociolinguist William Labov (1972) looked at the structure of spoken narratives in everyday talk in the USA and identified certain recurring features of what he called the 'western narrative'. Labov argues that western narratives have distinct stages (the sequence of which may vary) as follows:

Abstract	What is this to be about? This may summarise the point of the story, and is sometimes used as a way of taking the floor in conversation (this stage is optional)
Orientation	Who? When? What? Where?
Complication	What happened? This stage shows the sequence of main events and shows a crisis, or turning point
Evaluation	So what? This stage highlights the point of the story, and shows the speakers attitude to her/his story (evaluation is sometimes not a fixed stage, but happens throughout the narrative)
Result	What finally happened?
Coda	This stage is optional and might return listeners to the present (optional)

One of Patrick's other tapescripts suggested that some of his learners were able to produce a standard western narrative, albeit one which faltered in places. This extract took place during a one-to-one tutorial with a student, Victor. His narrative shows the features of Labov's as described above, i.e. abstract (Victor has difficulty writing), orientation (last year, tried to light a firework), complications (explosion and child getting burned, Victor lost a finger) and evaluation (provided by Patrick 'that's a terrible story').

Extract 2:
The firework
V = Victor, student;
T = Teacher (Patrick)

1. **T:** If you agree can you sign there please

    Asking V to sign ILP paperwork

2. **V:** Yes

3. **T:** Great

4. **V:** Already is difficult to writing and ... my finger is ...

    Unclear

5. **T:** Pardon?

6. **V:** Is already I got a problem in my writing and I have to use my finger it is more difficult to write

    Shows hand to teacher

7. **T:** Oh, oh really?

8. **V:** Yeah

9. **T:** Oh dear, so that makes it difficult for writing?

10. **V:** Yeah, some...is er hard writing, la.. last year ... I tried to... light it ... er ... a firework but it ... used to explode in my hand

11. **T:** Last year?

12. **V:** Yeah

13. **T:** Oh God

14. **V:** I lost my finger. Also I got some happening for my little child, child

15. **T:** How is your child?

16. **V:** He's just burning his back

17. **T:** Oh dear that's a terrible story

18. **V:** Yeah. I used to hospital for one week and I got er, operation

19. **T:** Oh

After working with Patrick's transcripts from his exploratory lessons, we concluded that his students needed explicit instruction and practice in how to structure and sequence narratives. They also needed classroom activities which would encourage interaction which was less vague and cursory than that produced by the topic card activity in Patrick's earlier lessons. The next part of the research cycle would therefore consist in trying to design lessons which would address these issues and help the students become more effective at telling the stories they wished to tell in English.

Telling stories: Lessons on narrative

First steps

In order to get ideas to help him plan a series of lessons to teach his learners to become more effective tellers of standard western narratives, Patrick used course books, teaching resource and books on methodology and the internet, which he found particularly fruitful, opting in the end to adapt material from the website **http://www.developingteachers.com**. Patrick adapted a series of lessons which aimed to make explicit to students the structure of spoken narratives and to give different situations in which to produce them.

The first lesson

The first lesson in the series was based on the theme 'The first time I did something'. The learners listened to a tape of a teacher talking about the first time she had taught English. They were asked to listen first for the gist of the story and then to focus on the structure, i.e. when and where did it happen, who was in the story, what happened, how did she feel? They were also asked to focus on discourse markers such as fillers and how the listeners show interest in the speaker's story. They were then asked to prepare a narrative of their own, explaining the first time they had done something themselves. For this, the students used a preparation sheet adapted from Labov's structure:

Where/When did it happen? Describe the situation.	Who else was in the story?
What happened?	How did you feel?
What vocabulary do I need?	What verbs do I need?
What can I do if I need to pause?	When I am listening how can I show: 1. interest: 2. surprise: 3. I don't understand:

(Jake Haymes, **http://www.developingteachers.com** accessed 5 November 2006)

The students were given 20 minutes preparation time and then asked to tell their stories to two different people, thus giving them a chance to tell their stories twice and to hear two different stories in return. At this point Patrick recorded the students speaking in pairs. Patrick writes the following:

From the transcripts of these recordings it was evident that although not all students recorded had developed the ability to tell their narratives in the structure outlined in the lesson, most had. Of those recorded, the majority seemed to be consciously telling their stories using the structure which the lesson had focused on. Other features looked at in the lesson were used to some degree, but not with the same level of success as the structural features. One immediate improvement which came to light was the apparent development of speaking ability after preparation time; a marked difference from the simple one-minute speaking activity used in the diagnostic lesson.

Here is an extract from one of the student narratives:

Extract 3: Baby cats
S = Salima; O = Odile

1.	**S**:	It was er about 20 years ago and erm (.) ah first	*Abstract*
		i want to speak about the first day (.) it was	
		about 20 years ago (.) my father's home and erm	
		(.) me and my sister er we we find some baby	
		cats in cellar and er	*Orientation*
2.	**O**:	Cats? Cats?	
3.	**S**:	Cats baby cats (.) They were very small and we	*Orientation*
		don't know how they erm (.) eat food we want	
		to feed them (.) and we every time (.) I think	
		maybe three times a day we put some milk in	
		the bowl [*laughs*] and we try to feed them (.)	
		they don't eat because they don't drink milk like	
		this in the bowl	
4.	**O**:	Yes maybe you need to (.) bottle like a child like	
		a baby	
5.	**S**:	Yes (.) me and my sister every time look at them	
		and we surprised why maybe they don't (.) they	
		didn't hungry maybe it's not a good time and we	
		try so many time but they didn't eat and we (.)	
		take their neck and er put in the bowl	
6.	**O**:	[*laughs*]	

7.	S:	Really [*laughs*] and I don't know after two days three days my father saw them and they (.) they every time they was very they was wet (.) they were wet whole the body 'cos we try to feed them and erm my father ask us what happened why they are like this (.) we said we try to feed them but they don't eat [laughs] (1 sec) but my father said the cat baby cat don't drink milk like this	*Complication*
8.	O:	They can't	
9.	S:	Yes (.) and my father think maybe we kill this cat my father put the cat on the road and their mother come and take them (.) after that we don't [*laughs*] look after any pets [*laughs*] we feel very silly every time I think about this sorry my god what they think [*unclear laughter or tears*]	*Evaluation and result*
10.	O:	But er you was child you were child and you don't know you didn't know	*Coda*

The second lesson

Having successfully got his learners to produce anecdotes with identifiable standard western narrative structures, Patrick decided to tackle the more problematic issue of practising narratives which might arise in the world outside the classroom, such as in job interviews. Research on job interviews (Roberts and Campbell, 2006) has shown that candidates are frequently expected to provide narratives in response to questions such as 'could you tell us about a time when you faced a difficult situation at work and how you overcame this?' Many ESOL learners may not realise that this question requires them to produce a narrative. They may understand the question but give a different kind of answer which is contrary to the expectations of the interviewer. Others may realise that this is what is required, but have problems producing narratives along the lines of those expected by native or more expert users of English.

Patrick again used a listening text to highlight the narrative structure, this time a home-made story of himself talking about a difficult situation in his professional life and what he did about it. As in the first lesson the students then spent time analysing the tapescript and preparing their own stories on a similar theme.

When he analysed the recordings from these lessons Patrick was pleased to see that the students were still producing successful narratives with an identifiable structure. However, the following problem had arisen:

Unfortunately, there seemed to be a lack of suitability in the topic chosen by students to cover in the second lesson narrative. Of those recorded none were to do with work, two were embellishments of the narrative developed for the first lesson, and the others didn't explain how the speaker had coped with the situation.

This left Patrick with a dilemma:

There was only one lesson left to teach before the three in the mini action research project were completed. I had the choice of looking at other features of spoken narratives and possibly teaching with another topic or interview question, or, as the second lesson had not brought about the results I was hoping for in terms of students' produced discourse, I could opt to re-tune the interview question I had and get students to focus more clearly on answering it. I decided to spend the final lesson focusing the students on answering the interview question again, in the hope that it would hone their standard western narrative skills to help in other narratives too.

The third lesson

In the last lesson of the action research cycle, Patrick changed his approach. He decided to focus first on real-life situations in which learners might have to produce narratives such as at college, in the bank, at the council offices, in conversation and in job interviews. He also decided to analyse questions from interviews which may require a narrative as a reply, focusing particularly on the question from the previous lesson ('Describe a time in your life when you had to deal with a difficult situation and say what you did to get over it') and language that might be used in describing how to solve problems, such as 'deal with an issue', 'try to control the situation', 'feeling pressured' and so on. Patrick then spent time helping students to choose an appropriate topic for the task.

The decision to focus on learners' own experience and the time given to discuss what might be needed as a response to certain questions in certain situations seemed to bring rewards:

Of the narratives produced there was a marked difference from the second lesson's in terms of detail, and student engagement with the question. Although far from perfect, the narratives told in this lesson were much closer to the makings of what I believe is a good answer to the interview question than in lesson two.

The following tapescript is part of a long narrative produced by an Iraqi woman student, Zuleyha, about a difficult time she had at work (it has been edited for length):

Extract 4: Angry parent
Z = Zuleyha; A = Aisha

1.	**Z:**	Er I am going to tell you a (.) er very difficult situation in my life (.) er which is about five years ago (.) er I remember er the first year when I taught children in a countryside (.)	*Abstract*
2.	**A:**	OK	
3.	**Z:**	Er it's not inside the city (.) in the countryside and which is very difficult because the people when they live there (.) you know they don't have (.) no education and er I taught children between eight nine and ten years (.) er at first you know it was difficult for me but the day after I felt better and er (.) but in my country er in the end of the year er every student they had they have to take exam to pass to another class er but er some problem happened to me because er one of them (.) not one of them lots of them er they don't (.) pass they didn't pass and er (.) when they went home after half an hour er (.) one of them came back with his father and er (.) he had a gun his father he had a **gun**	*Orientation* *Complication*
4.	**A:**	Oh no! It's dangerous	

5. **Z:** At first I had a shock I didn't know what to do I didn't know how to deal with but after er after I controlled myself (.) and er I didn't let him to get to me (.) I show myself I am confident and er I listened to him (.) I tried to calm down and explained his son the situation because er not just his son because a lot of student was er (.) were failed and they didn't come to me (2 secs) and er I tried a lot with him and I er I explained a lot of thing for him but er (.) er he didn't listen to me and I was (.) I was very scared **and er**

6. **A:** **Yeah** because it's stressful?

7. **Z:** It is stressful and er (.) all my body was shaking and I couldn't (.) I couldn't do anything you know to to er to end (1 sec) to end this problem then I tried to (.) er I went to my manager and I explained my problem and he said OK sit down in staff room and I am going to er to speak with him (.) and after my manager (.) he as well he couldn't do anything because he had a gun and it is very very difficult very dangerous (.) nobody can control this situation and after when he was (.) my manager he called police and they came they solve (.) they solve (.) they sorted out this problem but er it was very difficult for me because (.) I was a new teacher (.) I tried to calm it down I tried a lot of things to to deal with this problem but er but his father he didn't understand me (.) I show myself that I control (1 sec) but er that's all

8. **A:** **That's good control yourself**

9. **Z:** **But nothing** bad things happen (.) nothing   *Evaluation*
happen we try to control and that's all things
we can do

Conclusion – narratives

The above narrative might be too long and too dramatic to be entirely suitable for a job interview. However, this tapescript could very fruitfully lead to further discussion in future lessons about the suitability of certain stories for interview purposes (i.e. the level of drama and amount of explanation required in each context). The action research cycle which Patrick went through in his exploration of narrative structure with his learners shows several things. The first is that genres which have strong recurring features such as the standard western narrative are worth making explicit and analysing with ESOL learners. Making structures explicit through analysis of listening texts helps learners to focus on features of discourse which they may not have noticed in their day to day interactions.

The second thing shown here is the way that planning time and rehearsal can bring enormous benefits to the length and quality of learner talk. The benefit of sticking to the same structure for three lessons also brings benefits, despite Patrick's initial doubts that he could hold his learners' interests for so long. The final issue, which remained partially unresolved in Patrick's lessons, is the difficult one of dealing in the classroom with the real-life linguistic demands of the outside world. This inevitably means dealing with hypothetical situations and resorting to role-play, which many teachers and learners find unsatisfactory. However, Patrick has made a start here with his focus on learners' real-life reasons for needing to be able to produce narratives, and his focus on analysis of a realistic interview question.

Try it out

The following are steps you might follow if you want to try to work with standard western narratives:

■ In all lessons, if a student comes to the class with an urgent need to communicate something, allow her/him space and time to tell the story and work with that, or set aside a 15–20-minute slot on your lesson plan for students to talk, as Jim did in his lesson. Identify what kind of narratives they are struggling to produce, or what situations they face regularly in their daily lives in which narratives probably occur (e.g. in their jobs, conversations with neighbours, taking something back to a shop and so on).

- Give learners examples of narratives to listen to and analyse. These might be listening texts from existing materials or from the radio (Radio 4's 'Midweek' is a good source), TV or video, or you might want to record your own, your colleagues' or your students' narratives. A very effective way to get instant material is to record yourself as you tell a story and using the recording in class. You could then transcribe it for further analysis in future lessons. Ideas for the topic described in Patrick's lesson on doing something for the first time included: your first day at school/university/work; the first time you travelled alone; your first date; the first time you drove a car; your first English lesson. Think of other topics which might be a rich source of stories. Remember, stories do not always have to be dramatic or 'heavy'. Much of our everyday conversation is made up of fairly banal anecdotes which help us oil the wheels of our relations with others.

- Teach learners labels for the stages of standard western narratives as described by Labov, simplifying if necessary. Discuss if narratives are told differently in your learners' own languages/cultures, or if some questions such as an interview question would elicit a different kind of response to a narrative.

- In the next lesson invite learners to produce their own anecdotes. Give learners time to reflect, plan and rehearse their narratives and ask for one or two (or all if you have time) to tell their story in full class, or record them speaking in pairs/small groups.

- If necessary, provide opportunities for learners to develop the language they need to show active listening, e.g. 'Oh really?' 'That must have been ....'

- Identify what they need to help them be more effective in their communication, both as 'tellers' and listeners.

- Devise more lessons or activities based on your reflections on your learners' narratives; this genre lends itself perfectly to writing, for example, or you might look at more or less formal contexts and appropriateness. At a later stage, discuss the variations on Labov's model in sub-genres such as gossip.

And so on...

If you want to find out more

Labov, W. (1972) *Language in the Inner City*. Oxford: Basil Blackwell.

Thornbury, S. (2005) *How to Teach Speaking*. Harlow: Longman.

Thornbury, S. and Slade, D. (2006) *Conversation: From Description to Pedagogy*. Cambridge: Cambridge University Press.

Yuan, F. and Ellis, R. (2003) 'The effects of pre-task planning and on-line planning on fluency, complexity and accuracy in L2 and oral production', *Applied Linguistics*, Vol. 24(1): 1–27.

5 Turning talk into learning: Argumentation

They've got to this level in the language where they actually feel like they can express themselves in English which is something they couldn't do before. So it's nice to get them to be able to do that where they're actually saying what they think about something... they've got such strong opinions about absolutely everything so all you have to do is say a word and it will just spark off a whole discussion.
(Sarah, EEPP teacher)

Introduction

This section is about:

- how to set up discussions and debates in ESOL classrooms;
- helping learners to analyse different styles of argumentation, using tapescripts of their own discussions;
- raising awareness of the western academic style of argumentation and how it might differ from other styles;
- encouraging learners to reflect on the occasions they have to argue in their own contexts outside the classroom.

Discussion topics

As we discussed in section 2, there are many situations where learners themselves initiate talk in the classroom. This may sometimes lead naturally to a discussion or argument which we can usefully work with. There are also a lot of published and web-based materials which are concerned with finding suitable topics for discussion and ways to organise activities which maximise learner interaction, such as pyramid discussions and role-plays. There are fewer materials though on the linguistic and rhetorical skills required for argumentation, and it is this aspect of 'discussion' that we focus on later in this section.

Two types of talk in discussion lessons

Exploratory stage: James

We draw here on a series of lessons taught by Michael and one by James at Level 1 and Level 2 respectively. The extract we discuss here comes from a series of lessons in which James was trying out ways to get learners to produce different kinds of talk. In this particular lesson he set up a discussion. The topic is 'work' and the students have been introduced to some idioms relating to the topic. They have also listened to a tape of someone complaining about her boss. Prior to the discussion, James teaches his learners some language for disagreeing 'softly', such as 'yes, but...', 'I see what you mean, but...' and so on. He then sets up a pyramid discussion in which students are asked to think of seven qualities of a good boss, boil this down to four in negotiation with their partners and then in groups of four reduce the list to three good qualities. The final stage is the whole class deciding on the three most important qualities in a boss.

This extract is taken from the pair-work phase. The students are carrying out the task to a certain extent in the way that James had hoped. They engage in some mild discussion and are even seen to use the target structure 'I know what you mean but...' (the laughter suggests this is rather self-conscious!).

Extract 1: Good boss

1. **A:** I put fair
2. **B:** Yeah
3. **A:** Friendly
4. **B:** Yeah, I have that
5. **A:** Honest
6. **B:** Yeah, good honest
7. **A:** Er, intelligent, demanding
8. **B:** Why did you put demanding
9. **A:** Because your boss is not your friend at work, well, in my opinion, you should be friendly, if you have problem, you don't how to do it, er, but distant 'I'm your boss, and you are my employee'
10. **B:** Yes, I agree
11. **A:** I put this because you know erm sometimes boss can relation at work can be too familiar
12. **B:** I think you're right, yeah
13. **A:** But I think it's good when a boss is distant
14. **B:** maybe is good for in some place, but sometime you need to be more close with your boss and you can understanding what's your opinion, you have to know your boss very well otherwise you can't act proper, I think there will, would be a distance, but not that much and you know, you know you can't go so close with your boss. Everybody know there is a distance between the workers and boss. Yeah?
15. **A:** I know what you mean but [*laughs*]
16. **B:** [*laughs*]
17. **A:** However, um, if you, if there is this gap between you and your boss it's easier to respect each other
18. **B:** Of course, of course.
19. **A:** And he has more authority
20. **B:** Yes
21. **A:** Which is importance at work and er
22. **B:** OK, no problem.

However, this is one of the few examples from this activity in which the speakers negotiated with each other at all; all of the other talk was along the lines of 'what have you put? Yes me too'. This was a surprise to James who had been expecting a livelier disagreement. The lack of disagreement could be to do with the nature of the task and/or with the choice of topic, i.e. these learners naturally agree in this particular instance. Research on task-based pedagogy has shown that different tasks and topics produce different kinds of talk: for example, some tasks lead learners to diverge while others encourage them to converge. It is not always easy to predict which topics and tasks will encourage which types of talk; this is particularly true of discussions and one reason why they sometimes seem to produce different results than we expected. Another factor might be the nature of the culture of the classroom and the relations that develop between teacher and students and amongst the students themselves; it could be that some groups are more 'convergent' than others, and that some teachers (either consciously or unconsciously) foster a strong ethos of collaboration and collegiality in their classrooms. However, even though the results from this activity did not give James what he expected, it did show other types of talk such as collaborative and supportive talk, summarising and many examples of learners teaching each other new words and phrases.

"It is not always easy to predict which topics and tasks will encourage which types of talk"

Exploratory stage: Michael

Michael used a different activity in his exploratory stage which produced more divergent discussion. Again, this might be to do with the task itself, with the nature of the subject (a taboo topic for some publishers of global textbooks) and with the nature of the group. In this extract, Michael has given his students a set of cards with a list of 'controversial statements' such as 'Smoking should be banned in public places' on it. They have been given time to think about their opinions on one of the statements and to anticipate counter-arguments. They first present their opinions in mini-presentations and then engage in less planned debate with the others in the group. At this point, a discussion has begun about binge drinking:

Extract 2: Drinking

1. **D:** It's not good. And for health. For money. Everything is not good. Why? What have he drink for? Spend money? And just drink and go to the toilet and finish.

2. **B:** No it's the same as people that drinks orange juice **for**

3. **D:** **No**

4. **B:** Apple juice but why they don't drinks only water?

5. **D:** No no no because **only water**

6. **B:** **Yes they** choose. I get this choice. I can say OK instead of drink water maybe I could take one beer

7. **C:** I can **spend on cigarettes**

8. **E:** **But water** and orange juice health for your body

9. **D:** Yeah. And health for body

10. **B:** No. **Not**

11. **D:** **And mind** maybe

12. **B:** I understand what you think maybe but when you see some juice some juice in our supermarket just when I taste them I'm sure that's not good for my health because there are a lot of chemical inside or thing like that so (.)

13. **C:** To **be honest you can find a lot of chemicals**

14. **E:** **You can find you can find organic**

15. **C:** If you drink alcohol maybe is addict

16. **D:** But maybe affect another side **bad for health I suppose for mind**

17. **E:** **Absolutely unhealthy**

18. **D:** Professionals or everybody I don't think they drink anything

19. **C:** **I understand**

20. **D:** **Why** they lose their mind [*loudly*] Why? Why?

21. **C:** The problem is each time they take a little alcohol

22. **D:** Each time

23. **C:** they can enjoy this. This was even healthy for you

24. **D:** I don't think so. Because some better for mind maybe

25. **B:** Yes when you take a lot

26.	C:	If you're drinking every day it does much damage
27.	D:	Damage yeah
28.	C:	You're gonna lose everything and that's true because that alcohol is like really bad poison
29.	B:	Everything is bad in exaggeration it's like that's the same point that they say junk food junk food become dangerous when you eat hamburgers and fries every day but if you just eat hamburgers or pizza once a week or once in after in two weeks it should be not a problem but it becomes a problem if you eat it every day
30.	D:	But you maybe you can't control but just little bit you drink maybe more next time more more more [louder]
31	C:	[laughs] If you got the character like the person whose gonna be addict because this depends for your character it's not depends for alcohol for some people
32.	D:	No no alcohol because
33.	C:	Yeah but no some people they've got addict possibilities in theirs character and they will be easier to addict to alcohol or cigarettes because they've got something like this character in their brain
34	D:	Yeah

"One focus was the way these students structure their arguments and their rhetorical styles."

Analysis stage: Cross-cultural rhetoric

There were many things in this and the other extracts from Michael's class that would be worthy of follow up in future lessons. Here, however, we focus on one area in particular: the way these students structure their arguments and their rhetorical styles.

The study of rhetoric goes back as far as the ancient Greeks. Aristotle made a distinction between two different modes of argument: pathos, argument at the level of emotion, imagination and belief, and ethos, the speaker's capacity to be legitimate and authoritative. Cross-cultural rhetoric suggests that certain traditions argue from the basis of an appeal to authority: 'The law says so', and so on. In the western scientific tradition, authority isn't assumed; instead an argument builds up evidence to make a claim.

Both student B and student C use techniques which are more 'ethos' than 'pathos', and are closely allied to the style of argument in established western scientific tradition. Student B takes a specific example to make a general point: 'everything is bad in exaggeration' (turn 29). He makes a general claim (everything is bad if you do too much of it), and then backs it up with analogy. This is an example of arguing from a semantic generalisation, and is one which is regarded as 'classic' in western styles of argumentation. Student C uses a hypothetical structure, an 'if...then' argument (turn 26 and 31). He also acknowledges other peoples' views, then takes them on to back up his own argument.

For student D on the other hand, the argument is underpinned more by the pathos than the ethos mode of persuasion. He uses more passion than logic or rationalisation. More than the others, he invokes emotion to argue a case; this is seen through his use of repetition ('more more more' in turn 30), and the increase in volume as he speaks. Differences can also be seen in terms of varying levels and styles of collaboration in discussion. Students B and C are more collaborative in their arguments and pick up on one another's ideas, but student D repeats a point until he gains the floor.

The follow-up lessons: Language awareness

As a follow-up to this lesson Michael chose to focus closely on these learners' rhetorical styles. Rather than 'intervene' to attempt to get learners to change their styles (which may be neither desirable nor achievable) he chose to use an awareness-raising approach similar to Patrick's in section 4, but using the actual transcripts of the learners' own talk from the exploratory lesson. In order to help them do this, Michael provided a set of questions to focus them on the various features of their discourse and then invited them to discuss it with him and the other students. The questions were as follows:

Worksheet

Read the transcript carefully and think about the following questions. Look at how you try to persuade other people of your point of view. Think about these questions and make notes to help you:

How do you try to argue or persuade people?

- Do you persuade people using emotion and passion or do you try to use logic and reason?
- Do you use examples or evidence to support your argument?
- Do you use hypothetical situations to support your argument? (E.g. If you do this, then that will happen etc.)
- Do you try to make general points out of a particular example?
- Do you use what other people say to help you argue?

How do you help other people in discussion?

- Do you acknowledge other people's views?
- Do you listen carefully to what other people say?

How do you respond to what other people say?

- Do you interrupt other people or do you wait to take your turn? How do you decide when it is your turn to speak?
- Do you ask other people questions?
- Do you let them change the topic you talk about?
- Do you try to involve other people in discussion? How do you do this?

Accuracy

- Can you correct your own contributions?
- What happens in the transcript when you talk more? Do you make more mistakes? Is it more difficult to be accurate when you talk more? Is it more difficult to be persuasive?

- Is it better to talk less and make more contributions or to make fewer, longer contributions?

Culture

- How do you try to persuade somebody of your point of view in your own language and culture? Are there any rules? Is it different from how people do this in Britain?
- Can you think of any situations, outside the classroom, where you would need to persuade people to do something? Or when you have to argue with people? Write a list of situations: What problems do you think this might cause if English is not your first language?

General questions:

- How do people try to persuade each other of their points of view? Do they do this in different ways?
- How do people co-operate in this discussion? Do they ask each other questions? Do they help each other when they have difficulty with the language? Do they take turns to speak? How do the learners involve each other in a discussion?
- What do you think is important when trying to persuade somebody of your point of view?

In the discussion learners were able to identify aspects of their performance in terms of accuracy (how they became less accurate when talking under pressure), turn-taking (how it is sometimes difficult to know when you can take a turn) and interrupting and showing interest (through questions and back-channelling). They were also able to notice the different modes of argumentation that we describe above, such as use of hypothesis, generalisation, and giving evidence in the form of examples: 'I use examples to develop what I am saying'. There was also a discussion about argumentation based on passionate assertion and appeal to authority, and some put forward the view that this might be influenced by religion: 'some religion say it is allowed and some religion say it is not allowed or banned'. Paralinguistic features such as increasing volume, finger pointing and so on were also commented upon, and linked to an insistence that everyone comes into line with a particular viewpoint: 'he believes one thing and he thinks everybody should believe the same'.

The students then went on to apply their observations to the outside world, which Michael describes here:

> I asked learners to think of a situation outside the classroom where they had been forced to argue/persuade. I believe that modes of argumentation may become more crucial in formal encounters outside the classroom e.g. Job Centre interviews, Home Office interviews and so on.

> I asked learners to make notes on the context of the situation to ensure the activity was as authentic as possible and set up a role-play. I played the person in authority and they played themselves. By way of example, I role-played a situation with the ablest learner in the group. The learners not involved watched, thinking about modes of argumentation/listening and responding etc.

> The learners then carried out the role-play themselves. They commented later on the need to be 'firm but fair' and not to lose one's cool in encounters with officialdom and bureaucracy; to provide evidence, examples and supporting statements with reasoned argument. The potential consequences of passionate assertion were laid bare, as Student D, who epitomised the passionate, authority-based mode of argumentation was, again, passionate, waving his hands in a gesture that could have been regarded as confrontational and/or aggressive. It is one thing to raise awareness through meta-cognitive reflection, another to put the awareness into practice! This incident stimulated discussion on the way paralinguistic features, often culturally specific, can have significant implications for how ESOL learners may be perceived.

Conclusion – argumentation

Michael points out that 'teaching' western rhetorical styles was not his aim in any of these lessons:

> With regard to styles of argumentation, I feel that with something so embedded in cultural background and the socialisation process, something so closely intertwined with identity, it is difficult to speak of instant progress, or a before and after effect of teaching. Also, when dealing with styles of argumentation, we are, quite often, dealing with sensitive subject material/deeply held beliefs which people feel passionately about.

However, there are several reasons why it is worth raising the issues in this section with your ESOL students. Arguing like student D, for example, might lead to him being marginalised or dismissed by official organisations such as the Job Centre. Changing one's rhetorical style may not be either possible or desirable, but a chance to explore these issues in the classroom might lead to an awareness of why cross-cultural communication is sometimes fraught (a lesson which might of course equally be learned by expert English speakers in positions of power, but that is outside of the scope of this guide).

Another reason for a focus on argumentation is that students who wish to go on to do academic study will be expected to be able to argue, both in their essays and spoken contributions, in the accepted western academic style, i.e. providing evidence for their claims and finding flaws in the arguments of others.

Rather than expecting learners to adopt a style which is alien to them, or to turn into model 'westerners', the aim of Michael's lessons was to begin a process of awareness about discourse structures and rhetorical styles, thereby arming his students with analytic tools to better understand the interactions they engage in and to better develop their argumentation styles on their own terms.

"A chance to explore these issues in the classroom might lead to an awareness of why cross-cultural communication is sometimes fraught..."

Try it out

The following are steps you might follow if you want to try to work with argumentation:

- In all lessons: if a discussion naturally arises, allow space within the lesson for it to develop. Listen to students to find out their opinions and what they are interested in discussing. Encourage them to talk about current affairs and issues that arise in the international, national and local news.

- Set up a discussion activity which you predict will cause a divergence of opinion amongst the learners. This might come from a reading or listening text from existing materials or from newspapers, magazines, TV or radio. You could ask learners to provide their own topics, or set up formal debates. Decide on the amount of planning time students might need to decide on their opinions and think of counter-arguments.

- Record your learners having a discussion. Transcribe some parts of the discussion and discuss their rhetorical styles. You could use Michael's questions as a guide or design your own.

■ Give learners other arguments to analyse from other sources. These might be listening texts from existing materials or from the radio, TV or video. Try to get examples of people employing different rhetorical styles.

■ Devise more lessons or activities based on your reflections on your learners' argumentation. This might be role-plays of situations in which arguments might occur, in different contexts and with different speakers and hearers.

■ At high levels use written arguments such as newspaper articles or academic essays and identify how arguments are made. Encourage students to analyse different aspects to arguments such as making a claim and providing evidence. Give them examples of arguments with fallacies and ask them to identify them. There are many resources for this in the field known as 'critical thinking'.

And so on...

If you want to find out more

Roberts, C., Jupp, T. and Davies, E. (1992) *Language and Discrimination: A Study of Communication in Multi-ethnic Workplaces.* London: Longman.

Toulmin, S. (1969) *The Uses of Argument.* Cambridge: Cambridge University Press.

Wooffitt, R. (1996) 'Rhetoric in English'. In: J. Maybin and N. Mercer (eds) *Using English: From Cambridge to Canon.* London: Routledge.

Critical thinking: **http://www.criticalthinking.org.uk** (activities for A-level students, has many examples of arguments and fallacies, etc.).

Conclusions

This action research suggested many things about working with ESOL learner talk, some of which we include below.

- The main message emerging from both the EEPP and this action research project is that when learners speak 'from within', the language they produce is more complex and more memorable than that which results from controlled practice. If you don't do anything else, we suggest that this is one thing you could explore with your learners.

- Even at beginner levels it is possible to focus on talk in interaction beyond the level of word or short utterance. Learners need to interact and use longer chunks of language from a very early stage, so this should not be postponed until later in the curriculum.

- There are many valuable sources of information about spoken language which come from outside the sources we usually draw on for teaching and learning language, e.g. sociolinguistics (in the case of Labov and narrative in section 4) and philosophy and critical thinking (in section 5).

- There is much more happening in ESOL classrooms than the learning of linguistic forms. How to present yourself, persuade, entertain and inform require an understanding of how to be part of a social group and how to act in certain ways. ESOL classrooms are an important site of second language socialisation.

- Learners are a real resource, and in fact often know more about many things than their teachers. All communication requires some 'gap' in knowledge or understanding, so the stories they tell from within are genuine communicative acts.

- Teachers do not have to be actively in control all the time. It is fine to let go of your lesson plan and let learners take up or choose the topic. Giving the control of the topic over to learners means they are more likely to listen to each other and get involved in interaction.

"This means being flexible, taking risks and changing habits."

■ Finally, changing your teaching means being prepared to try out new things, or doing things in different ways. This means being flexible, taking risks and changing habits which you may have formed over a long time. However, as you learn about your learners and their talk, you are also exploring and getting to know more about your own practice, and developing your own personal pedagogical theory. The long-term benefits of this may be of crucial importance through your teaching career, as this quote from Denise Ozdeniz (1996) suggests:

Practitioners capable of investigating their own classrooms...are no longer at the mercy of policy changes or paradigm shifts...[they] are empowered to control how they incorporate new ideas into their teaching as opposed to having new ideas forced upon them. (p.123)

References

Allwright, D. and Bailey, K.D. (1991) *Focus on the Language Classroom: an introduction to classroom research for language teachers.* Cambridge: Cambridge University Press.

Auerbach, E.R. (1992) *Making Meaning Making Change.* USA: Centre for Applied Linguistics and ERIC.

Baynham, M. (2007) 'Agency and Contingency in the Language Learning of Refugees and Asylum Seekers', Special Issue *Linguistics and Education*, Vol. 17(1): 24–39.

Baynham, M., Roberts, C., Cooke, M. and Simpson, J. (2007) *Effective Teaching and Learning: ESOL.* London: NRDC.

Block, D. (2003) *The Social Turn in Second Language Acquisition.* Edinburgh: Edinburgh University Press.

Cameron, D (2001) *Working with Spoken Discourse.* London: Sage.

Carter, R. (2003) 'The grammar of talk: spoken English, grammar and the classroom', in: *New Perspectives on Spoken English in the Classroom.* London: QCA.

Condelli, L., Wrigley, H. S., Yoon, K., Seburn, M. and Cronen, S. (2003) '*What Works' study for Adult ESL literacy students.* Washington, DC: US Department of Education.

Cooke, M. and Roberts, C. (2007) **Reflection and Action in ESOL Classrooms.** London: NRDC.

Graddol, D., Cheshire, J. and Swann, J. (1994) *Describing Language* (2nd Edition). Milton Keynes: Open University Press.

Klippel, F. (1984) *Keep Talking: Communicative Fluency Activities for Language Teaching.* Cambridge: Cambridge University Press.

Kumaravadivelu, B. (2003) *Macrostrategies for Language Teaching*, Yale University Press.

Labov, W. (1972) *Language in the Inner City.* Oxford: Basil Blackwell.

Maryns, K. (2005) 'Displacement in asylum seekers' narratives'. In: M. Baynham and A. de Fina (eds) *Dislocations/Relocations: Narratives of Displacement*. Manchester, UK St Jerome.

McNiff, J. and Whitehead, J. (2005) *Action Research for Teachers: A Practical Guide*. London: David Fulton Publishers.

Ordeniz, D. (1996) 'Introducing innovations into your teaching'. In: J. Willis and D. Willis (eds) *Challenge and Change in Language Teaching*. Oxford: Heinemann.

Roberts, C. and Campbell, S. (2006) *Talk on Trial: Job Interviews, Language and Ethnicity*. London: DWP.

Roberts, C., Jupp, T. and Davies, E. (1992) *Language and Discrimination: A Study of Communication in Multi-ethnic Workplaces*. London: Longman.

Seedhouse, P. (2005) *The Interactional Architecture of the Language Classroom: A Conversation Analysis Perspective*. Oxford: Blackwell.

Thornbury, S. (2005) *How to Teach Speaking*. Harlow: Longman.

Thornbury, S. and Slade, D. (2006) *Conversation: From Description to Pedagogy*. Cambridge: Cambridge University Press.

Toulmin, S. 1969 *The Uses of Argument*. Cambridge: Cambridge University Press.

Tsui, A.B.M. (1995) *Introducing Classroom Interaction*. London: Penguin.

van Lier, L. (1996) *Interaction in the Language Curriculum: Awareness, Autonomy and Authenticity*. Harlow: Longman.

Wallace, M. J. (1998) *Action Research for Language Teachers*. Cambridge: Cambridge University Press.

Walsh, S. (2006) *Investigating Classroom Discourse*. London: Routledge.

Wooffitt, R. (1996) 'Rhetoric in English'. In: J. Maybin and N. Mercer (eds) (1996) *Using English: From Cambridge to Canon*. London: Routledge.

Yuan, F. and Ellis, R. (2003) 'The effects of pre-task planning and on-line planning on fluency, complexity and accuracy in L2 and oral production', *Applied Linguistics*, Vol. 24(1): 1–27.

Zuengler, J. and Cole, K. (2004) 'Language socialisation and second language learning'. In: E. Hinkel (ed.) (2004) *Handbook of Research in Second Language Teaching and Learning*. New Jersey: Lawrence Earlbaum Associates.